Paul
Follower of Jesus

by

B. A. Ramsbottom

2008

Gospel Standard Trust Publications
12(b) Roundwood Lane
Harpenden,
Hertfordshire
AL5 3BZ
England

Published by:
Gospel Standard Trust Publications

ISBN : 978-1-897837-82-5

2008

Printed in China by:
Hung Hing Off-set Printing Co., Ltd

Paul's Early Days

There was once a little boy whose name was Saul. He lived in a busy town called Tarsus, not far from the seaside.

Saul was not a naughty boy. In fact, he believed he was very good. He knew there is a God, and was proud he was a Jew, one of God's chosen people. But there was something very, very sad. Saul did not love Jesus.

As he grew up, Saul heard about Jesus. But he was angry. He did not like Him. He did not believe He was God's Son and he did not like those who loved Jesus. He hated them.

So what do you think he did? It was terrible. When he became a man, he did everything he could to hurt the Christians, those who were followers of Jesus. He tried to get them put in prison – and prisons were not nice places in those days. Often they were cold and dark and miserable.

But something worse! He was glad when they were killed. What had they done wrong? Nothing. They just believed Jesus was God's Son and loved Him.

Have you heard of Stephen? He was a really good Christian man, but Saul's friends were cruel to him. Stephen loved Jesus; but they threw big stones at him till he fell down dead. And what do you think Saul did? He

helped them. He looked after the clothes of these wicked men who were throwing stones at poor Stephen.

But before Stephen died, he looked up to heaven and said he could see Jesus there. He even prayed for the cruel people who were killing him.

We wonder what Saul thought? Some nasty pricking thoughts about it all! But can you believe it? He still wanted to go on, fighting against Christian people.

But now something amazing! Saul was going to be a follower of this Jesus that he hated, and he would travel all over the world telling people what a wonderful Person Jesus is.

But first of all, something must happen, mustn't it? Saul's life must be changed. But it seemed impossible. Saul loving and following Jesus? God was going to do it. For God can do anything, however impossible.

You can read about this in the Acts of the Apostles, chapter 7, verses 54 to 60, and chapter 8, verses 1 to 3.

Paul's Conversion

Where are all these people going? They are travelling along an old road from Jerusalem to a place called Damascus. It was a long, lonely road. How they were travelling we do not know – perhaps on horses or camels, or some walking. But we know they were going to get hold of the Christians there, tie them up and throw them into prison.

And who is that at the front? Saul – and you can tell he is very angry. He would like to kill the lot of them! And he thought he was serving God!

But something wonderful is about to happen – a miracle. A bright, dazzling light is shining in the sky, brighter than the sun. Saul falls down, helpless. He is blind.

But a noise can be heard. What is it? The people think it is thunder, but Saul can hear a voice. It is the voice of God. It is speaking to him. It says, "Saul, Saul." It asks him, "Why are you persecuting ME?" Saul knows it is God's voice. He is frightened. He cries, "Who art Thou, Lord?"

And then Saul received the biggest shock of his life. The voice says, "I am Jesus." So Jesus is God! The one he hates and has been fighting against is God.

R.G

Saul's life was never the same again. God's grace had changed it. What do you think? Do you think Saul still went on to seize hold of the followers and friends of Jesus, and put them in prison? Never!

Shaking, terrified, Saul asked what he must do. And the voice of Jesus from heaven told him to go into the city of Damascus, and he would find out. So he got up from the ground. But he could not see, so someone had to hold his arm and lead him into the city.

What had happened? Saul was one whom God had chosen, and now God's almighty grace had changed his life – for ever. Even his name was changed to Paul. There never was a more loving follower of Jesus than God's servant Paul.

You can read about this in Acts, chapter 9, verses 1 to 9 (and also chapter 22, verses 3 to 11, and chapter 26, verses 4 to 21).

Preaching About Jesus

In the old city of Damascus lived a man named Ananias. He was one of God's people. He was a Christian.

One day he could hear God speaking. But he was amazed! God was telling him to go and find a man called Saul. And He told him where to find him.

Poor Ananias was terrified. He knew all about Saul. He was coming to seize hold of Ananias and his friends, and throw them into prison. "Not Saul?" thought Ananias.

But God said, "Yes. I have chosen him. He is different. He is going to be a preacher. He is sorry for what he has done."

So Ananias quickly did what God had told him. He went and found Saul. And he spoke so kindly to him.

Poor Saul! How sorry he is for his sins! But now he knows who Jesus is, and he is trusting Him. Jesus has forgiven him. Now Ananias puts his hands on Saul's head and, wonderful, he can see again.

Immediately he is baptized – to show that his life is changed: he now knows and loves the Lord Jesus.

As soon as he can go out, he tells people that Jesus is the Son of God. He knew that, didn't he? He had looked up and seen Him in heaven and heard His voice.

And now the whole of Saul's life was going to be preaching about Jesus as the only way to be forgiven and to get to heaven. Saul could have said:

"There was no other good enough
To pay the price of sin;
He only could unlock the gate
Of heaven, and let us in."

Everyone was amazed. They could hardly believe it. Is this really Saul? What has happened?

Saul's old friends did not know what to say. They knew something strange had happened. So what do you think they did? They tried to kill him.

In an exciting way Saul escaped and left Damascus. Do you know what Saul's new friends did? They got a big basket, Saul climbed inside it, and they let it down over the city wall by a rope. Cities in those days had big stone walls all round them.

So Saul went on his way. But he was a very different Saul. The grace of God had changed him.

But many people could not really believe it was true. It seemed impossible. This terrible man, who hated God's people, was he really different? People were still frightened of him.

At last he came back to the city of Jerusalem. This is where he had started from. The Christians were terrified.

But there was a very kind man there called Barnabas. He made friends with Saul. You know how nice it is to have a good friend. He looked after Saul, and told his own friends all that had happened to Saul on the way to Damascus – the light from heaven, the voice, everything. A miracle had happened.

At last the Christians at Jerusalem were happy with Saul.

You can read about this in Acts, chapter 9, verses 10 to 28 (and also chapter 22, verses 12 to 21).

Paul's Journeys

Paul (as we now call him) dearly loved the Lord Jesus. From now on he spent his whole life travelling about telling people about this wonderful Saviour he had found. They needed to be sorry for their sins, to confess them, and ask to be forgiven, and he told them of this wonderful Saviour Jesus.

We wonder how he travelled – for he went hundreds of miles. Was it by donkey? or camel? or walking? We know sometimes it was in a ship crossing the sea.

Some people listened. Some did not. Sometimes God performed wonderful miracles when Paul preached.

On one little island where Paul went, a wicked man called Elymas tried to stop him. He was a wizard. But God struck him blind. He could not see. But the chief man on the island loved Paul and what he said, and believed.

God gave Paul power to perform miracles. At one place called Lystra there was a man who had poor, lame feet. Even when he was a little boy he could not walk. How sad! But by the power of God Paul made him walk. See the poor man now, not just walking but leaping for joy.

So now the people thought Paul must be God. They were throwing flowers round his neck. They were worshipping him. It all made Paul very, very sad. He said, "No. Only God is to be worshipped. I am not God."

But what do you think is happening next? What a change! They are all throwing stones at him, trying to kill him, just as Stephen was killed. Someone has told them Paul is *not* a god. He is a bad man. Have they forgotten the wonderful thing that happened to the poor lame man? I am sure *he* was not throwing stones.

Now the stones begin to hit Paul. He falls down. Has he been killed? Is he dead? People think so.

But no! He gets up, and goes off with his few friends. And what do you think he did? He still went on telling the people about Jesus – in the next city, and another, and another.

Paul was never happy unless he was speaking about Jesus, telling how He lived, and died on the cross, and rose again, and lives in heaven, an Almighty Saviour.

You can read about Paul's journeys in Acts, chapters 13 and 14.

More of Paul's Journeys

It would take too long to tell about all Paul's travels preaching about the Lord Jesus. What weary miles he went! Often he was tired, cold, hungry, thirsty – sometimes attacked by robbers.

Once he and one of his friends were cruelly beaten by a prison-keeper. Their poor backs were sore and bleeding. But what do you think they did? Cry? Grumble? No, they sang hymns of praise to God.

And in the middle of the night God sent an earthquake. Everything began to shake, and the prison doors flew open. Paul could easily have got away. But he didn't.

But now what is happening? The cruel prison-keeper is speaking kindly to him. He is frightened. He is sorry. He knows he has done wrong. And he begs Paul to tell him how he can be saved. Paul's answer was clear:

"Believe on the Lord Jesus Christ, and thou shalt be saved."

But what a miracle! The prison-keeper is different. See, he is tenderly bathing Paul's wounds. Now he is giving him something to eat in his own house (for Paul must have been hungry). But above all he is confessing

that he is trusting in the Lord Jesus, and he is baptized. How Paul must have rejoiced!

Another time Paul went to the great city of Athens. The people thought they were all very wise and clever, but Paul was very sad because they did not know anything about the true God. So Paul told them who the true God is, and all about the Lord Jesus, and the need to be sorry for their sins and to turn to Him.

As always, some believed – others didn't. But God's work went on.

Another time Paul went on preaching for such a long time till it was the middle of the night. No wonder that one poor young man fell asleep. He was called Eutychus. He was sitting up in a window. What a strange place! So it is not surprising that he fell down.

He was dead. But by God's power, Paul performed a miracle, and brought him back to life.

So day after day, month after month, year after year, Paul went on teaching and preaching. But he wanted to go back to Jerusalem – where he started out on his journeys.

You can read about these journeys in Acts, chapters 16 to 20. Paul himself mentions them in 2 Corinthians, chapter 11, verses 23 to 28.

Back to Jerusalem

It was a long, long time since Paul had been at Jerusalem. His friends were so pleased to see him. Especially they were glad to hear of all his adventures and how God had been with him.

But soon poor Paul was in trouble again. Once more he was thrown into prison. What had he done wrong? Again, nothing, but tell the people about Jesus.

Some wicked men even made a plot to kill Paul. But strangely a young boy heard all about it. We don't know anything about this boy except that Paul was his uncle. He was pleased to help his uncle Paul. He told the chief of the Roman soldiers, who made sure that no harm could come to him.

Then one important man and another important man wanted to hear all about him. What had he to say? What had he done? One was called Felix; the other was called King Agrippa. Again and again Paul said, "I have done nothing wrong. I have only told people about Jesus – that He is the Son of God – that He died – that He is alive again."

In the end Paul said he would like to be judged by the great Emperor himself. His name was Caesar. Now Caesar lived in Rome – so off to Rome Paul had to go.

You can read about this in Acts, chapters 21 to 26.

The Shipwreck

To get to Rome Paul had to travel in a ship over the sea. But if he had had adventures before, there was none like this.

Have you ever seen a terrible thunderstorm? The wind has howled. And the rain has pelted down. It is frightening. Or have you ever been on a boat when the sea is very, very rough? As Paul sailed, the ship came into a dreadful storm. It lasted day after day. For a long time it was pitch dark. No one could see anyone else. At night there was no moon or stars.

The sailors were terrified. They thought they would all be blown into the sea and be drowned. There was just one man calm and peaceful – Paul. He was not frightened. Why? God had spoken to him, and told him *not* to be frightened. No harm would come to him. God was with him.

But even more! Though there were nearly three hundred people on board the ship, not one of them would be drowned.

Day after day, for two weeks, their ship was thrown about here and there in the storm. Would it never end? But at last they wondered if they were near land.

Then suddenly – a tremendous crash! Whatever is happening? The ship has been smashed, and is broken into pieces. All of them were thrown into the sea. Those who could swim struggled to the land. Those who could not swim got hold of pieces of wood and boards that had broken off from the ship, and floated to the shore. It must have been horrible – drenched through, cold and shivering.

But through God's mercy they were all safe. Not one was drowned.

You can read about this in Acts, chapter 27.

Melita

Wherever were they? What was this place? What sort of people would they meet? Paul and all the crew must have wondered. Some of them must have been frightened.

It was a little island called Melita. The people looked wild and savage – but no, they were very kind. See what they are doing! Lighting a fire so that Paul and the poor shivering sailors and prisoners and others can get warm. How kind!

But what is happening now? A terrible thing! When the fire was lit, there was a snake among the sticks that were put on the fire. Suddenly it shot out and seized Paul's hand.

Everyone was horrified. Some said, "He must be a bad man. He has escaped being drowned, but he is still going to die."

All eyes were looking at Paul. But he shook the poisonous snake back into the fire – and to everyone's amazement, he was all right. They were all thinking he would drop down dead. Now they were all saying, "He must be a god."

For about three months they all went on living there. Paul spent his time praying for the people, especially those who were ill, and God made them better.

I am sure that he also told them about the Lord Jesus and His power to save.

You can read about this in the last chapter of the Acts of the Apostles, chapter 28, verses 1 to 10.

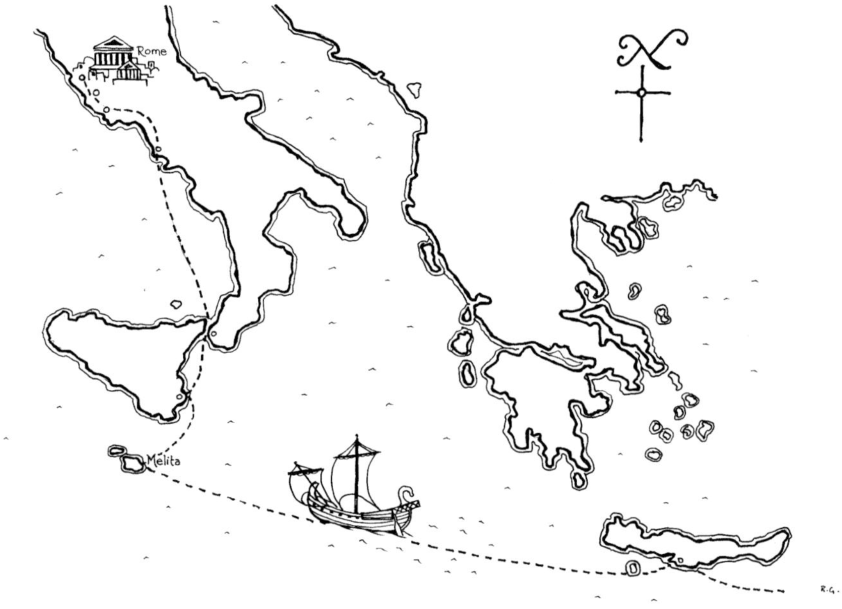

The End

At last it was time for Paul to leave the little island and be taken on his way to Rome. I should think they were all sad to see him go, wouldn't you? And he would have so many things to think about.

This time they sailed along calmly and quietly. Their ship was called *Castor and Pollux.* We should like to hear all about their journey, but nothing is told us.

Then there was a long journey by road to Rome. Would it be on horseback? How glad Paul must have been when a few who loved the Lord Jesus came to meet him! Do you know what he did? He thanked God.

At last the long journey ended. Paul had reached the great city of Rome. He was allowed to live in a little house. But a soldier guarded him. And he was fastened to the soldier by a heavy chain. It must have been very uncomfortable.

People came to see him. Some believed what he told them about Jesus. Some didn't. But Paul knew what he believed, and he knew the Lord was with him.

The Bible does not tell us any more. It was two long years before Caesar would hear him. At last his enemies killed him. But Paul was not afraid. He knew that through the grace of the Lord Jesus he was going to heaven.

We should like to know more about the end of Paul's life, shouldn't we? But the last thing the Bible tells us about him is that in Rome he was preaching about the Lord Jesus. I think that is how Paul would like us to remember him, don't you?

You can read about this in the closing chapter of the Acts of the Apostles, verse 11 to the end.

R.G.